Spider Monkey

by Dee Phillips

Consultants:

Dr. Christina J. Campbell
Assistant Professor of Anthropology, California State University, Northridge

Kimberly Brenneman, PhD
National Institute for Early Education Research, Rutgers University, New Brunswick, New Jersey

BEARPORT
PUBLISHING

New York, New York

Credits
Cover, © Roland Seitre/Nature Picture Library; 2–3, © Roland Seitre/Nature Picture Library; 4–5, © Adrian Hepworth/NHPA/Photoshot; 7, © Michael & Patricia Fogden/Minden Pictures/FLPA; 8, © Thomas Marent/Minden Pictures/FLPA; 9, © Adrian Hepworth/Alamy; 10, © Roland Seitre/Nature Picture Library; 11, © Dave Irving; 12, © Jurgen & Christine Sohns/FLPA; 13, © Nick Gordon/Nature Picture Library; 14, © mypokcik/Shutterstock, © Tristan Tan/Shutterstock, and © Timur Kulgarin/Shutterstock; 15, © Nick Gordon/Nature Picture Library; 16, © Eric Isselee/Shutterstock; 17, © Gerry Ellis/Minden Pictures/FLPA; 18, © Adrian Hepworth/NHPA/Photoshot; 19, © Roland Seitre/Nature Picture Library; 20–21, © kerstiny/Shutterstock and © David Tipling/FLPA; 22, © Ruby Tuesday Books; 23TL, © Michael & Patricia Fogden/Minden Pictures/FLPA; 23TC, © Nick Gordon/Nature Picture Library; 23TR, © Andrey Pavlov/Shutterstock; 23BL, © David Tipling/FLPA and © Mark Herreid/Shutterstock; 23BC, © Janelle Lugge/Shutterstock; 23BR, © KYTan/Shutterstock.

Publisher: Kenn Goin
Editorial Director: Adam Siegel
Creative Director: Spencer Brinker
Design: Emma Randall
Editor: Mark J. Sachner
Photo Researcher: Ruby Tuesday Books Ltd

Library of Congress Cataloging-in-Publication Data

Phillips, Dee, 1967–
  Spider monkey / by Dee Phillips.
    p. cm. — (Treed: animal life in the trees)
  Includes bibliographical references and index.
  ISBN-13: 978-1-61772-912-6 (library binding) — ISBN-10: 1-61772-912-4 (library binding)
  1. Spider monkeys—Juvenile literature. I. Title.
  QL737.P915P45 2014
  599.8'58—dc23
                              2013011501

For more information, write to Bearport Publishing Company, Inc., 45 West 21st Street, Suite 3B, New York, New York 10010. Printed in the United States of America.

10 9 8 7 6 5 4 3 2 1

Contents

Breakfast Time

In a tall tree, a black-handed spider monkey spots some fruit.

The juicy food is just out of reach, however.

To grab it, the hungry monkey wraps its long tail around a branch.

Dangling from the tree, it picks the tasty fruit with its hands.

Then the monkey eats its breakfast high above the ground.

There are several types of spider monkeys, including black-handed spider monkeys. Each kind sleeps, finds food, and raises its babies in trees.

tail

black-handed
spider monkey

fruit

A Treetop Life

Spider monkeys live in **rain forests**, where it's warm and rainy.

They spend all their time in the highest branches of the tallest trees.

The monkeys live in groups called **communities**.

The members of a community include adults, young monkeys, and babies.

How do you think spider monkeys got their name?

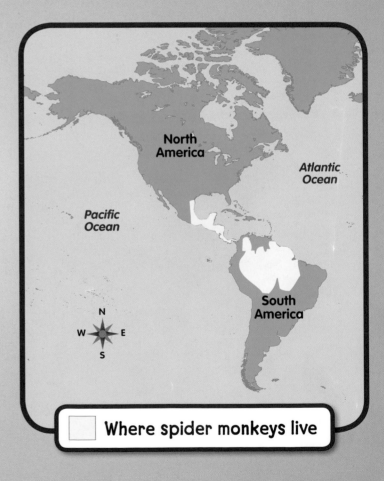

North America

Atlantic Ocean

Pacific Ocean

South America

N
W · E
S

Where spider monkeys live

Black-handed spider monkeys live in groups that have about 20 to 40 members.

Meet a Spider Monkey

All spider monkeys have long arms and legs, and a long tail.

Together, these body parts look a little like a spider's long legs.

Spider monkeys have red, black, and brown fur.

Some kinds, however, also have patches of white fur.

tail

spider monkey

Black-handed spider monkeys have black skin on their hands and feet. Their fur is pale brown, reddish-brown, or black.

black-handed spider monkey

How do you think spider monkeys move through the trees?

Moving Through the Trees

A spider monkey usually moves through the forest by swinging from tree to tree.

First, it grabs a branch with one hand.

Then it swings its body to grab the next branch.

Sometimes, a spider monkey uses both its arms and its legs to move along branches.

Other times, it stands up and walks— just like a person.

tail

A spider monkey can also swing by using its strong tail like a third arm. The end of the monkey's tail has no fur, which helps it grip slippery branches.

Day and Night

At night, a group of spider monkeys sleeps high in a tree.

As the sun rises, the group splits into small groups of five or six monkeys.

Each group spends the day moving through the treetops.

The monkeys look for food, eat, rest, and **groom** each other.

As night falls, the entire group comes together again to sleep.

spider monkey resting

What foods do you think spider monkeys eat?

young spider monkey
grooming its mother

Spider
monkeys groom
each other's fur
to remove dirt
and **insects**.

Time to Eat

A spider monkey's main food is juicy, **ripe** fruit.

It also eats leaves, flowers, nuts, and seeds.

Spider monkeys often hang from branches by their tails or feet when eating.

This keeps their hands free for gathering food.

Spider Monkey Food

fruit

flowers

leaves

A spider monkey can also hang from a branch by its hands and grab food with its tail.

A Baby Monkey

A female spider monkey **mates** with a male monkey from her group.

About seven and a half months later, she gives birth to a baby.

The little newborn monkey can't swing, walk, or take care of itself.

The baby stays close to its mother by holding on to her fur.

When it's hungry, the baby drinks milk from its mother's body.

baby
spider monkey

mother

baby

All black-handed spider monkeys are born with black fur. As they grow, their fur may change to reddish-brown or pale brown.

Riding and Playing

At first, a baby spider monkey moves through the trees by clinging to its mother's chest.

When it's two months old, it's strong enough to ride on her back.

At three months old, the baby starts to eat fruit.

Soon, the little monkey begins to swing and play in the trees on its own.

It stays close to its mother, though, and jumps on her back when she moves.

baby spider monkey

As they grow older, baby monkeys meet up with other babies in their group to play. They swing, climb, and chase each other through the trees.

Growing Up

A young spider monkey drinks its mother's milk until it's about two years old.

Then it's ready to eat only adult food and take care of itself.

A male spider monkey stays with his mother's group for his whole life.

At four years old, a female spider monkey goes to live with a different group.

Now she is ready to mate and have her own treetop baby.

eight-month-old spider monkey

An adult black-handed spider monkey is about 18 inches (46 cm) long from its head to its bottom. It weighs between 13 and 20 pounds (6 and 9 kg).

Imagine you are a scientist watching spider monkeys for a whole day. Write down all the things you might see the group doing.

Science Lab

Spider Monkey Show-and-Tell

Use clay and pipe cleaners to make a model of a spider monkey.

Then collect some leafy twigs and hang your monkey from them.

Present your model to friends and family members. Explain how the monkey swings from branch to branch using its long tail and arms.

How to Make a Monkey

1. Use modeling clay to make the spider monkey's body and head.

2. Bend a pipe cleaner to make the monkey's long arms. Then press the arms into the monkey's body and squeeze the clay around the arms to hold them in place. Attach another pipe cleaner in the same way to make the monkey's legs.

3. To make the monkey's tail, push a pipe cleaner into the back of the monkey's body.

Science Words

communities
(kuh-MYOO-nuh-teez)
groups of monkeys that
live together

groom (GROOM) to clean
another animal's fur

insects (IN-sekts) small
animals that have six legs,
two antennas, a hard covering
called an exoskeleton, and
three main body parts

mates (MAYTS) when a male
and female come together in
order to have young

rain forests (RAYN FOR-ists)
places where many trees and
other plants grow, and lots
of rain falls

ripe (RIPE) soft and ready
to eat

Index

Read More

Dunn, Mary R. *Spider Monkeys.* Mankato, MN: Capstone (2013).

Gosman, Gillian. *Spider Monkeys (Monkey Business).* New York: Rosen (2012).

Lunis, Natalie. *Howler Monkey: Super Loud (Animal Loudmouths).* New York: Bearport (2012).

Learn More Online

To learn more about spider monkeys, visit **www.bearportpublishing.com/Treed**

About the Author

Dee Phillips lives near the ocean on the southwest coast of England. She develops and writes nonfiction and fiction books for children of all ages. Dee's biggest ambition is to one day walk the entire coastline of Britain—it will take about ten months!